THE 60-MINUTE GROWTH PLAN

HOW A SINGLE SHEET OF PAPER CAN CHANGE YOUR BUSINESS AND THE WORLD

JOSHUA NUYEN

A room without books is like a body without a soul.

— Marcus Tullius Cicero

PREFACE

It's easy to become extremely busy and yet ultimately unproductive because all you do is spin your wheels but get nowhere. To avoid that, you need to plan how to move things forward – or more accurately, you need a simple and fast planning process that works. Most planning processes are too complicated to be of much use in the real world. A better approach is to set aside one hour for developing your business growth plan and the strategy you want to use. On a single sheet of paper, you want to answer the only three questions that count when it comes to planning growth in any endeavor:

1. Where do you want to go?
2. Where are you now?
3. How will you get from here to there?

Once you learn how to run a 1-hour planning session and produce a 1-page plan for growth, you're then equipped with everything you need to take your business to the next level again and again. The process is breathtakingly simple:

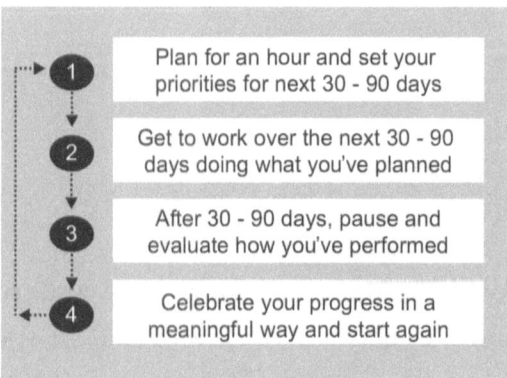

"An effective growth planning system is the best indicator of whether your business will grow. It's time to develop your plan and learn a system that will serve you for the rest of your life. No matter where your business is today, you can grow it through this system. You'll also develop your own leadership skills, not through classroom training, but through the process of setting, achieving and celebrating progress on your priorities."

– Joe Calhoon

1
THE 1-HOUR PLANNING PROCESS

Traditional business planning takes too long, doesn't engage everyone and usually produces materials which sit on a shelf gathering dust. Instead of that, get everyone involved in a one hour planning session which centers on three key questions:

Planning doesn't happen a lot of the time in companies for five main reasons:

- Most planning sessions generates documents which are too long to be of any practical use.

- Many people see endless planning sessions as being a complete waste of time. Rather than trying to make them more effective, they instead classify all planning as a waste of time.
- When too few people are engaged in planning how to grow your business, planning becomes an event for the elite rather than something everyone does.
- All too often, planning generates documents which never get used. They sit on the shelf gathering dust rather than getting earmarked and applied.
- Complicated plans often have little or no impact on organizational performance. There is a disconnect between what the plan says and what people do in their day-to-day jobs.

To avoid these problems, there is a better way forward. Have a planning process that is so straightforward it can be completed in an hour and then everyone gets back to work. Instead of generating a document, generate a single sheet of paper which people can use in their everyday decisions. And keep everything simple by focusing on the key issues involved.

The outline for a 1-hour planning session is:

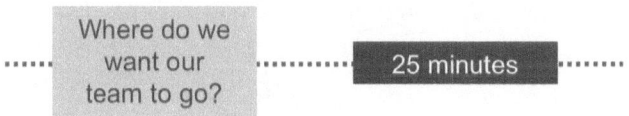

Spend the first 25 minutes refining and fine-tuning your long-term plans. This will involve spending some time on four elements which provide the stable core of your business.

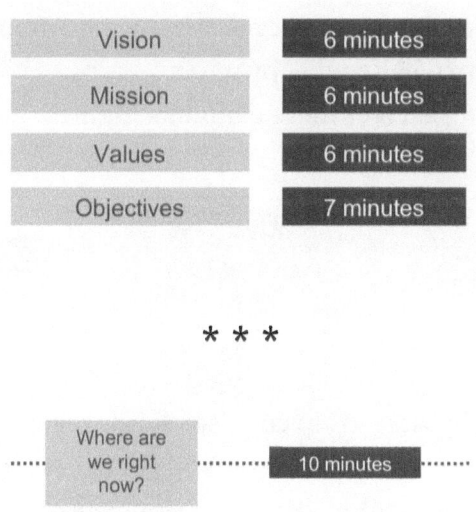

* * *

Allocate the next 10 minutes to facing the brutal realities of where you are at the present time and identifying all of the big issues which must be addressed in order for you to move forward. This is the time where you cut through the clutter and clarify which items you need to focus on to have the greatest impact.

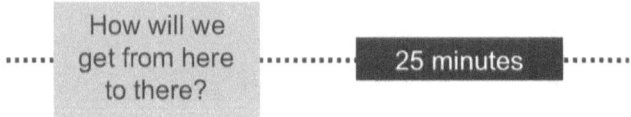

In the last segment of your planning session, you figure out your strategies which determine the course you're planning on following and your priorities – who will do what by when.

Taking each of these elements in turn:

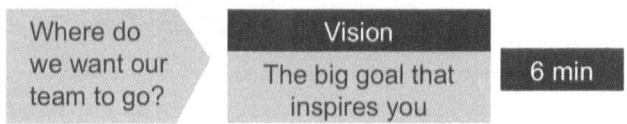

Your vision is a concise word picture which describes your organization's ideal future. It should be inspiring and at the same time measurable and achievable. Take this time to write or to improve your organization's vision statement. Some examples:

"To be the worldwide airline of choice." – Delta Airlines

"To be the world's premier food company, offering nutritious, superior tasting foods to people everywhere." – Heinz

"To treat our team with respect, our guests as family, and to offer the finest barbeque experience in the country." – Jack Stack Barbeque

* * *

To write your own vision statement, come up with answers to four fundamental questions:

1. How good do you want your organization to be?
2. What are you providing, in terms of specific products and services.
3. Which customers or which markets do you serve?
4. What is the geographic scope of your business?

Once you answer those four questions, you can then polish and refine your vision statement to come up with something you find inspiring and highly motivational.

- "We are Kansas City's most trusted provider of telecom solutions."

- "Our vision is to become the premier provider of innovative online marketing solutions to businesses in the Midwest."

Note the best visions are always measurable. There is a specific number you're aiming at. That number can vary according to the nature of your business and might be gross revenues, profit, revenues per employee or whatever other metric is most applicable. Having a hard measure as an integral part of your vision is helpful because it can be used to gauge success, to choose one path over another and to otherwise optimize your operations.

* * *

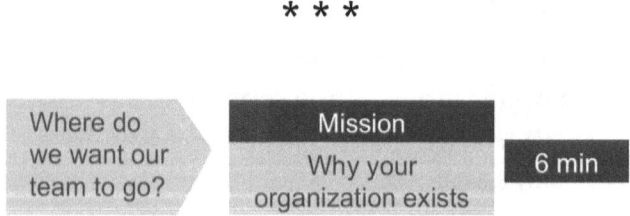

Mission is the contribution you're aiming to make to your customers' lives. It is a clear and compelling statement why your organization even exists. A clear and concise mission statement will be a tool to help everyone stay focused on what's important. Some examples:

- "To organize the world's information and

make it universally accessible and useful." – Google
- "To create memories that last a lifetime." – Cruise Holidays of Kansas City
- "To make people who are away from home feel like they are among friends and really wanted." – Marriott
- "To build a motor car for the great multitude. It will be so low in price that no man making a good salary will be unable to own one and enjoy with his family the blessing of hours of pleasure in God's great open spaces. Everyone will be able to afford one, and everyone will have one." – Ford Motor Company

To write your first draft of your own mission statement, think about the value you provide to your customers and complete this statement: "Helping our customers …" Some ideas:

- "Helping our customers choose their ideal vehicle."
- "Helping our customers plan for and provide for their retirement."
- "Helping our customers enjoy a stress-free experience by providing them with a reliable and safe rental vehicle."

Peter Drucker suggested a good mission statement should be concise enough to be able to be printed on a T-shirt. The challenge is to come up with something which is not only short but also compelling and intensely motivational for the people inside your company. Above all, ensure your mission statement is customer focused and centered. Great organizations exist to serve their customers.

> *"The best way to predict your future is to create it."*
> *- Stephen R. Covey, founder, FranklinCovey*

* * *

| Where do we want our team to go? | **Values** — Your standards of behavior | 6 min |

Values define your standards of behavior and your code of conduct. Values help your team gel because they articulate how your team members will treat each other and the customers you serve. Values always drive your organization's performance and results.

> "We are committed to providing our employees a stable work environment with equal opportunity for learning and personal growth. Creativity and

innovation are encouraged for improving the effectiveness of Southwest Airlines. Above all, employees will be provided the same concern, respect, and caring attitude within the organization that they are expected to share externally with every Southwest customer."

"Focused, friendly, fun and fair."
– J. Schmid

To write your own values statement, start by choosing between three and seven of these possibilities:

- Accountability – answer for your results
- Commitment – superior standards of achievement
- Creativity – produce original ideas and thoughts
- Excellence – engage our best efforts
- Fairness – to be free from any biases
- Fun – to foster an environment of playfulness
- Integrity – to be counted on to do what you say
- Loyalty – to use difficult situations as opportunities
- Passion – to have exceptional enthusiasm
- Respect – to esteem the abilities of others

- Responsibility – to know and do what's expected
- Service – to meet the customer's expectations
- Teamwork – to work together productively
- Positive attitude – to be helpful and constructive
- Life/work balance – to hit a good balance
- Generosity – to give freely of your time and talents
- Empowerment – to enable others to choose and act
- Friendly – to be favorably disposed

"I look for three things in hiring people. The first is personal integrity, the second is intelligence, and the third is a high energy level. But, if you don't have the first, the other two will kill you."
— Warren Buffett, CEO, Berkshire Hathaway

* * *

| Where do we want our team to go? | Objectives — Measures and metrics of success | 7 min |

Objectives are measures of your success and your organizational performance. Objectives may be customer measured, employee measured or financially measured.

To write your objectives:

1. Determine what you will measure. Keep it simple and straightforward.
2. Specify how you will measure it. This may take some time to get right so be patient.
3. Describe specifically where you want to head for each measure.

For example, your objectives chart may look something like this:

	What to measure	How to measure	Objective
Cust	Customer satisfaction	Two question survey	70 +
	Market share	% of business	60%
Emp	Productivity	Revenue / employee	$150,000
	Employee satisfaction	Assessment questionnaire	3.2
Finan	Gross revenue	Annually	$1.5M
	EBITDA	Annually	$200,000
	Debt	Dollars	0

"Too often we measure everything and understand nothing. The three most important things you need to measure in a business are customer satisfaction, employee satisfaction and cash flow."
– Jack Welch, former CEO, General Electric

* * *

| Where are we right now? | Face the facts and identify the big issues to address | 10 min |

The 80/20 principle suggests there is always an inbuilt imbalance between inputs and outputs in your business. What you're trying to do in this 10 minute long session is to zero in on the most important issues facing your business at the present time. Or put another way, you're trying to identify the 20 percent of your issues which will directly lead to 80 percent of your future growth.

So how do you do that? In practice, there are only eight generic categories of business issues. Within each category, there are three specific issues which crop up again and again. You should:

1. Go through the list and come up with a list of five to ten major issues which must be addressed in order for you to grow your business.
2. Once you've written down those major issues, go through and rank them in order of importance.
3. Starting with your most important issue first, sit down and start thinking about what strategy would directly address and resolve that issue for you. Keep that

strategy list handy because you'll need it soon.

"Leadership does not begin with vision. It begins with getting people to confront the brutal facts and to act on the implications. One of the primary ways to demotivate people is to ignore the brutal facts of reality."
– Jim Collins, author

"Most businesspeople, including your competitors, don't take the time to plan well. It's a weakness for them – and an opportunity for you. They are rightly concerned that a strategic plan will take days or weeks to develop – and who has that kind of time. The 1 Hour Plan for Growth solves this problem by capturing the essence of the planning process in a way that takes about an hour of your time. It provides a quick introduction to a lifelong leadership tool."
– Stephen R. Covey, founder, FranklinCovey

"It does not take much strength to do things, but it requires a great deal of strength to decide what to do."
– Elbert Hubbard, philosopher and writer

Category	Issue
Human Resources (Your people)	Untrained employees who are unable to do their jobs effectively
	Lack of a system of accountability for results
	Low levels of employee engagement in the business
Physical Resources (Your equipment or physical space)	Inadequate or outdated technology
	Lack of proper equipment for the jobs at hand
	Underutilized space which increases overheads
Financial Resources (Your access to capital)	Lack of timely, accurate financial statements
	Insufficient cash reserves
	Inadequate budgeting system
Profit Requirements (Your ability to generate a profit)	Costs are increasing faster than projected
	Inconsistent pricing policy leaves money on the table
	Lack of internal expense controls
Innovation (Your products and services)	Aging product line which needs to be refreshed
	Less than acceptable levels of service quality
	Too few streams of income to ride out ebbs and flows of sales
Marketing and Sales (Your sales channels)	Lack of in-house sales skills
	Underutilization of social media as a sales channel
	Outdated brand in need of revamp
Productivity or Delivery (Your delivery infrastructure)	Too much rework being required on products sold
	Ineffective handoff between sales and support
	Too many mistakes are being made at our customer call centers
Social Responsibility (How you give back to the community)	Overall lack of team spirit or esprit de corps
	No consistent program for giving something back to the community
	Lack of involvement with worthwhile causes

| How will we get from here to there? | Develop the strategies which will move you forward | 15 min |

S trategies are the high-level choices you make which determine the courses of action your company will follow in the months ahead. As a general rule of thumb, having five good strategies will likely give you enough to be working on at any one time.

Strategies are the most important part of your growth plan for a number of reasons:

- Strategies provide a focus on the areas where you need to work in order to grow your business.
- Strategies provide the pathways you need to follow in order to reach your vision and fulfill your mission.
- Strategies get all your employees engaged and better serving customers.

A good template for a business strategy is:

| Specify the end you have in mind | By / Through | Clarify your strategic choices |

- Improve our work environment by increasing our physical space and investing in better state-of-the-art office technology.
- Increase levels of employee engagement by making sure the right people are in leadership positions and by revamping

and upgrading our employee rewards program.
- Increase our financial stability by obtaining a line of credit from the bank and by expanding our enterprise's capital base.
- Enhance our potential and capacity for growth through exploring the possibilities of greater bank financing and greater employee ownership.
- Maximize our operational efficiency by utilizing our available resources efficiently and by integrating best-in-class technology, developing scalable business systems and by enhancing our in-house lines of communication.
- Create ravings fans out of our customers by providing them with the best dining experiences they've ever had bar none.

Usually the best way to develop your strategies is to sit down and develop your own strategy matrix. An example of a strategic matrix for human resource issues is something like this:

Human Resources		
End in Mind	By / Through	Strategic Choices
Build a high performance team		Hire better qualified people
Expand our capacity to serve		Put the right people into the right positions
Increase employee engagement		Run leadership training programs
Strengthen our management team		Provide better in-house training resources
Improve employee retention		Rotate people into various managerial positions
Recruit more high performers into the sales team		Increase and improve our incentives program

Once you have your strategic matrix in place, you can mix and match to come up with workable and appropriate strategy choices. From this matrix, some possibilities are:

- Build a genuine high-performance team by revamping and improving our various hiring and training programs.
- Build a sales superstars team by increasing our incentives and by offering more ongoing in-house training resources and opportunities.

For each of the big issues facing your company which you've identified, you should now develop a strategy matrix for that area and brainstorm some creative strategy options. Come up with viable strategies which will address that big issue and position your company advantageously so you can grow.

> *"The experienced mountain climber is not intimidated by a mountain – he is inspired by it. The persistent winner is not discouraged by a problem – he is challenged by it. Mountains are created to be conquered; adversities are designed to be defeated; problems are sent to be solved."*
> – William Arthur Ward, author

> *"Plans are nothing; planning is everything."*
> – Dwight Eisenhower, president of the United States

> *"Good leaders create a vision, articulate the vision,

passionately own the vision, and relentlessly drive it to completion."

– Jack Welch, former CEO, General Electric

"Management by objectives works if you first think through your objectives. 90% of the time you haven't."

– Peter Drucker, father of modern management

"You can't talk yourself out of a problem you behaved yourself into."

– Stephen R. Covey, founder, FranklinCovey

"My job is to turn over rocks and look at the squiggly things, even if what you can see can scare the hell out of you."

– Fred Purdue, former vice president, Pitney Bowes

"There is nothing as useless as doing efficiently that which should not be done at all."

– Peter Drucker, father of modern management

"It is very difficult to lead today when people are not really participating in the decision. You won't be able to attract and retain great people if they don't feel like they are a part of the authorship of the strategy."

– Howard Schultz, CEO, Starbucks

"Profit in business comes from repeat customers, customers that boast about your product or service, and bring their friends with them."
– W. Edwards Deming, author and consultant

* * *

| How will we get from here to there? | Set out tasks to be accomplished and assign to people | 10 min |

Once you've decided on your strategies, all that remains is to set priorities – to specify which specific tasks will be assigned to which individuals. Most growth plans forget about priorities which is unfortunate because:

- Priorities provide a point of focus for people to achieve the important tasks which will grow your business.
- Priorities are an opportunity for people to enhance their character, to deepen their character and to build confidence.
- Priorities can set out the specific actions which are required to deal with organizational issues.

The basic template for a growth plan priority is:

Start with a verb → Make it measurable → End with a date → Assign to a person

1. *Start with a verb* – which ideally shows complete actions. Good verbs to use include "Finish", "Complete", "Make" or "Debrief".
2. *Make it measurable* – or observable. You have to be able to tell when the priority is done. If you cannot, then it's not specific enough. If you can tell when something is completed, then you can also tell how much progress you've made.
3. *End with a date* – because high-performance organizations value action over paralysis. Target completion dates are also a great way to prioritize and deliver accountability.
4. *Assign the priority to one person* – who will own the task and ensure it gets completed. That person doesn't have to do everything themselves but they're accountable for the job to get completed.

A few examples of priorities:

- Greg will hire a new salesperson by June 14.

- David will upgrade the Website by July 4.
- Steven will debrief the events team by January 31 to come up with ideas on how to achieve a 10% increase in direct marketing leads next year.

Priorities are the missing element in most business growth plans. They're an essential component because they take grandiose sounding growth strategies and translate them into everyday actions. Priorities also close the loop in that they specify who will be accountable for the results generated further down the road.

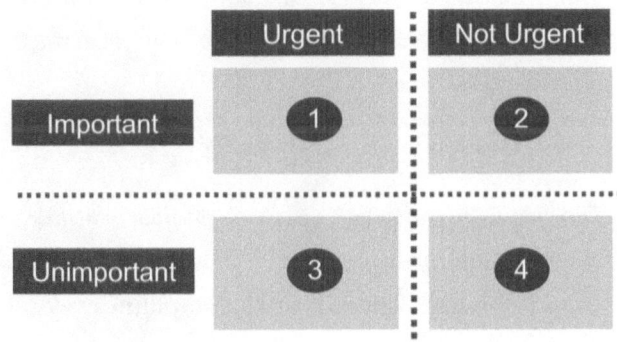

It's fairly well known business activities in general can be classified into four quadrants depending on urgency levels and importance levels. Most people fall into the trap of spending the majority of their time engaged in activities which are in quadrants 3 and 4. By developing a business growth plan which has growth strategies linked through to priorities, you increase the odds you'll spend more time in quadrant 1 and quadrant 2 business activities. That can make a sizable difference.

> *"During the 1990s, I had the privilege of serving as a senior consultant with the Franklin Covey Company. I spent the entire decade helping people discover habits and principles of effectiveness that could improve their organizations and their lives. Stephen Covey told me that the most important advice he would give a person in the area of time management was to plan your week – every week – before it even begins. Likewise, The 1 Hour Plan for Growth helps you develop a business plan before you even start investing your time."*
> – Joe Calhoon

> *"The key is not to prioritize what's on your schedule, but to schedule your priorities."*
> – Stephen R. Covey, founder, FranklinCovey

> *"Don't be a time manager, be a priority manager."*
> – Denis Waitley, author

> *"Of all the things I've done, the most vital is coordinating the talents of those who work for us and pointing them toward a certain goal."*

– Walt Disney, founder, Disney

"Profit is not the legitimate purpose of business. The legitimate purpose of business is to provide a product or service that people need and to do it so well that it's profitable."

- James Rouse, entrepreneur and philanthropist

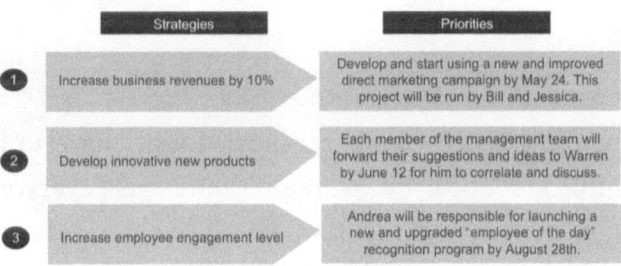

2

THE 1-PAGE PLANNING DOCUMENT

Your plan to grow your business doesn't have to be complicated. To be workable and get everyone engaged and working towards the same end, you should be able to boil your plan down to one page which deals with the three time frames of action:

- Long-term – 5 to 25 years – what is your organization's big and inspiring goal (your vision), what contribution do you want to make (mission) and what standards will help your team work together (your values).
- Mid-term – 1 to 3 years–what are your measures of success (your objectives) and what paths will you take to get there (your strategies)

- Short-term –30 to 90 days–who will do what and by when (your priorities).

Capture all these six elements on a single sheet of paper everyone has and understands and you have in place a plan for growth which people can and will use because they understand what you're doing.

The real strength of 1-hour planning is it makes your business growth plan come to life. A good way to keep the plan current is to follow this kind of pattern:

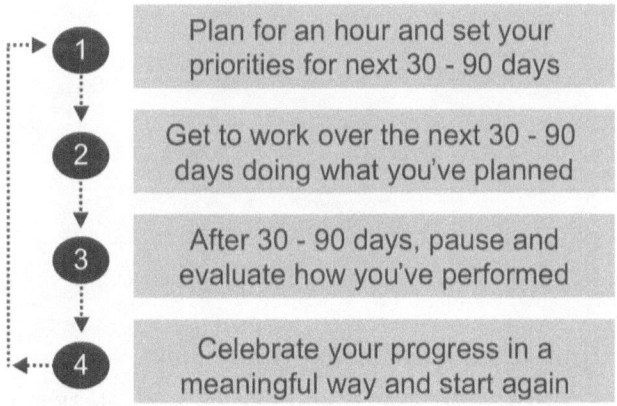

Once a year you might bring everyone together and make updates as required to your vision, mission, values and objectives but most of the time, getting together for one hour of planning every few months to reset priorities and celebrate progress will work very well. It will keep everyone on the same page.

To get more done in less time, embed an action plan right into your growth plan. An action plan is a list of specific steps along with due dates and the person who will be responsible. The underlying logic is:

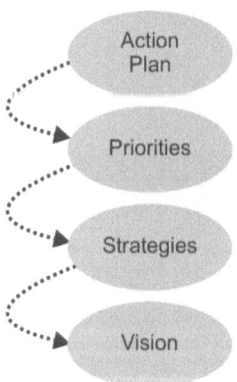

Your action plan helps you achieve your priorities. Priorities help you achieve your strategies and your strategies help you achieve your vision. By embedding a viable action plan right into your 1-page growth plan, you make it easier for everyone to be more productive because they know what needs to be done daily.

* * *

The other good thing about this action plan approach is you get just the right amount of project oversight this way. It's all too easy for managers to go to either extreme – to try and micro manage everything themselves or to abandon employees and leave them to their own devices.

Ideally, you want to hit a balance between these extremes. You want employees to be trusted but at the same time accountable for what they do. By developing an action plan in this way, you specify what needs to be done, set milestones for the project and then step back and let your people go to work. You can check in periodically to see how things are going. The person who is responsible can show the progress they've made and you can then provide the support and encouragement which is required. In all, action plans enable managers to hit a good balance.

Best of all, 1-hour planning sessions and 1-page growth plans are practical enough so you can engage your entire team in the planning process. This has numerous flow-on benefits:

- Everyone gets to understand your vision, mission, values and objectives. You're all on the same page and pulling in one

direction rather than working at cross purposes.
- By involving everyone in your planning sessions, you're building bench strength and leadership skills.
- Since the planning approach is simple, everyone will be in a position to contribute their best ideas. There won't be the perception business planning is something only the senior management team do.
- You can create periodic events where you celebrate progress towards key objectives. This can build a great team spirit.
- 1-hour planning is a great way to run monthly management meetings as well. You can:

    - *Review progress.*
    - *Share stories about lessons learned.*
    - *Identify emerging issues.*
    - *Discuss your people and operations.*
    - *Look for new and emerging growth opportunities.*
    - *Set new priorities for the month ahead.*

"*The journey of a thousand miles begins with one step.*"
   – Lao Tzu, Chinese philosopher

"The elevator to success is out of order. You'll have to use the stairs ... one step at a time."
  – Joe Girard, author

"A person must grow out of small problems to free up the energy to deal with bigger problems. That is the process of growing and maturing. The same applies to organizations."
  – Ichak Adizes, Corporate Lifecycles

"If the rate of change inside an organization is slower than the rate of external change – the end is near."
  – Jack Welch, former CEO, General Electric

"Free market capitalism works better when more people understand how free enterprise works and their role."
  – Joe Calhoon

"Inside every old company is a new company waiting to be born."
  – Alvin Toffler, writer and futurist

Arnie's Pizza's Plan For Growth (example):

THE 60-MINUTE GROWTH PLAN

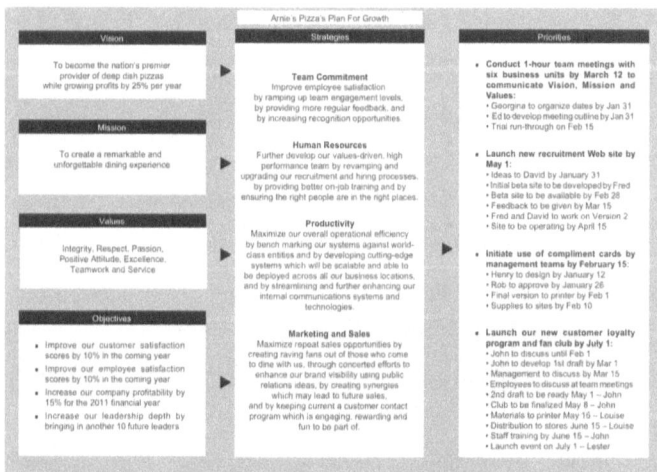

Now it is your time to fill in yours!

www.ingramcontent.com/pod-product-compliance
Lightning Source LLC
Chambersburg PA
CBHW031513210526
45464CB00007B/2893